Pebble® Plus

Wild About Wheels
CONSTRUCTION
Vehicles

by Kathryn Clay

Consulting Editor: Gail Saunders-Smith, PhD

Consultant: Rita Branca Leahy, PhD, PE
Technical Consultant, California Asphalt
Pavement Association

CAPSTONE PRESS
a capstone imprint

Pebble Plus is published by Capstone Press,
1710 Roe Crest Drive, North Mankato, Minnesota 56003
www.capstonepub.com

Library of Congress Cataloging-in-Publication Data
Clay, Kathryn, author.
Construction Vehicles / by Kathryn Clay.
    pages cm. — (Pebble plus. Wild about wheels)
Summary: "Simple text and full-color photographs describe eight differerent vehicles used in construction work"— Provided by publisher.
 Audience: Ages 4–8.
 Audience: K to grade 3.
 Includes bibliographical references and index.
 ISBN 978-1-4914-2117-8 (library binding) — ISBN 978-1-4914-2358-5 (ebook PDF)
 1. Earthmoving machinery—Juvenile literature. 2. Construction equipment—Juvenile literature. I. Title.
 TA725.C54 2015
 629.225—dc23   2014032591

Editorial Credits
Nikki Bruno Clapper, editor; Janet Kusmierski, designer; Tracy Cummins, media researcher; Laura Manthe, production specialist

Photo Credits
Shutterstock: aarrows, Design Element, Alexandr Shevchenko, 11, Blanscape, 9, Dmitry Kalinovsky, 15, Cover, Faraways, 7,
21, smereka, 13, TFoxFoto, 5; Thinkstock: gece33, 19, Toa55, 17.

Note to Parents and Teachers

The Wild About Wheels set supports national curriculum standards for science related to engineering
design, forces and interactions, and structure and properties of matter. This book describes and illustrates
construction vehicles. The images support early readers in understanding the text. The repetition of words
and phrases helps early readers learn new words. This book also introduces early readers to subject-specific
vocabulary words, which are defined in the Glossary section. Early readers may need assistance to read
some words and to use the Table of Contents, Glossary, Read More, Internet Sites, Critical Thinking
Using the Common Core, and Index sections of the book.

Printed in the United States of America in Stevens Point, Wisconsin.
092014   008479WZS1

Table of Contents

Big Builders

Construction vehicles
load, lift, push, and dig.
These giant machines help
workers build roads, bridges,
and buildings.

Loaders

Dump trucks haul heavy

loads of dirt and rock.

Drivers stay safe in the cab.

cab

Concrete mixers take

concrete to building sites.

Concrete stays soft in the

spinning drum.

drum

Lifters

How do workers build

skyscrapers? Cranes lift

heavy pieces into the air.

A crane's boom can hold

the weight of five elephants.

boom

Pushers

A bulldozer's blade
pushes dirt and rocks.
Two tracks help the vehicle
move across bumpy ground.

blade

track

Road rollers help workers pave new roads. A heavy drum flattens hot asphalt mixed with other materials.

drum

Graders use long blades to flatten land. Some graders push snow off roads.

blade

Diggers

Backhoes are like

two machines in one.

The bucket digs up dirt

and rocks. The loader

carries away the dirt.

loader

bucket

19

Breakers

Workers sometimes need
to get rid of huge rocks.
Rock breakers smash rocks
into small pebbles.

Glossary

asphalt—a thick, dark liquid that is often mixed with sand and gravel to make paved roads; asphalt hardens as it dries

blade—a wide, curved piece of metal on a machine; the blade pushes, scrapes, or lifts rocks and dirt

boom—the metal arm of a crane

concrete—a mixture of cement, water, sand, and gravel that hardens when it dries

construction—the act of building something

drum—a turning container that mixes concrete; the heavy round presser of a road roller

haul—to pull or carry a load

pave—to cover a road or other surface

track—a metal belt that runs around wheels; a bulldozer uses two tracks to move over bumpy ground

vehicle—a machine that carries people and goods

Read More

Doman, Mary Kate. *Earthmovers and Diggers.* All About Big Machines. Berkeley Heights, N.J.: Enslow Publishers, 2012.

Kawa, Katie. *Bulldozers.* Big Machines. New York: Gareth Stevens, 2012.

Parrish, Margaret. *Trucks and Diggers.* Wild Rides. Mankato, Minn.: New Forest Press, 2012.

Internet Sites

FactHound offers a safe, fun way to find Internet sites related to this book. All of the sites on FactHound have been researched by our staff.

Here's all you do:

Visit *www.facthound.com*

Type in this code: 9781491421178

Super-cool stuff!

Check out projects, games and lots more at
www.capstonekids.com

Critical Thinking Using the Common Core

1. Which construction vehicle helps workers pave roads? (Key Ideas and Details)

2. What is a track? What kind of construction vehicle travels on tracks? (Craft and Structure)

Index

Word Count: 150
Grade: 1
Early-Intervention Level: 20